UP FAITH!
God loves a faith that is always looking up

DEACON LARRY ONEY

Up Faith! God loves a faith that is always looking up
Written by Deacon Larry Oney
Copyright © 2013 Deacon Larry Oney

ISBN: 149042573X
ISBN-13: 978-1490425733

DEDICATION

To my mother, Beatrice Allen, who's life helped to shape my own faith in Jesus Christ. I will always love you mom!

CONTENTS

LETTER TO THE READER

Dear Reader,

This book can be used as a personal reflection/spiritual growth book or with small groups. Each day a Scripture is highlighted that discusses faith. A short reflection is offered followed by contemplation questions related to the Scripture of the day. The last piece for each day are personal reflection questions—things to reflect on personally.

Up Faith! God loves a faith that is always looking up is for this time and season that is upon us—we are constantly under attack from the Enemy about our faith and have to decide where we will take a stand and what side we will be on. This is a time for action!

I pray that this book is a blessing in your life and that God's grace and peace surround you while you meditate on the gift of faith that God gives to His children.

In Christ,

Deacon Larry Oney

PART ONE:

Faith as a Response to God

DAY 1
FAITH NOT SEEN

Faith is the realization of what
is hoped for and evidence of
things not seen.

Hebrews 11:1, NAB

Reflection:

There are many types of faith…many things in this world that we have faith in during our life. One of the simplest examples of faith in our day-to-day lives is the stop light. When we are stopped at a red stop light and that light turns green, we have faith that the cars going in the opposite direction are going to stop because their light has turned red. Since we have faith that this will happen, we begin driving when our light has turned green.

While this is a simple example of faith, it gives a clear example of what it means to have faith in something. This kind of faith could be called "experiential faith" because it was developed over time experiencing the light turning green.

Christian faith also has a component of experiential faith—God invites us into a relationship with Him and we experience that relationship with Him and that is what draws us deeper into the faith. "…Faith is man's response to God, who reveals himself and gives himself to man, at the same time bring man a superabundant light as he searches for the ultimate meaning of his life…" (CCC 26)

So faith is our response to God. In *Porta Fidei*, Pope Benedict XVI wrote:

> To profess faith in the Trinity—Father, Son and Holy Spirit—is to believe in one God who is Love (cf. 1 *Jn* 4:8): the Father, who in the fullness of time sent his Son for our salvation; Jesus Christ, who in the mystery of his death and resurrection redeemed the world; the Holy Spirit, who leads the Church across the centuries as we await the Lord's glorious return.

What we profess to believe or have faith in is our response to God's invitation to us. God invites us to believe and we have faith in God as we experience Him, even if we cannot see Him.

Contemplation Question(s):

What is faith? Why does faith have anything to do with "things not seen?"

Faith is hope, love, trust.

Things we can not see in our lives we have a positive outlook that in this will it will all be ok. NO MATTER THE OUTCOME!

Personal Reflection:

What do you hope in today? What or whom do you place your faith? What builds your faith?

I hope in today for those who do not know you to soften their hearts. To be open to you. Hope in the future for my kids and my husband.

DAY 2
BLESSED FAITH

Those who have faith are
blessed along with Abraham
who had faith.

Galatians 3:9b, NAB

Reflection:

As we respond to God and enter into a relationship with God we are blessed. We are blessed by just being with God—connected to God. God's grace covers us and God's protection is extended over us.

One Scriptural example of this concept of blessing can be found in the story of the Prodigal Son (Luke 15:11-32). One son took his inheritance and squandered it while the other son stayed with his father and worked. When the younger son returned in disgrace the father welcomed him and was happy to have him back. When the older brother questioned his father about throwing a feast for his brother, the father replies simply, "My son, you are here with me always; everything I have is yours." (Luke 15:31b)

When we are in relationship with God, everything that He has is ours. We have full access to all that is God's. We have His council to depend on, His wisdom to learn from, His protection, and His grace.

Contemplation Question(s):

In Galatians 3:9, who are blessed along with Abraham?

Personal Reflection:

Do you have faith? How are you blessed because of your faith?

DEACON LARRY ONEY

DAY 3
SENT FAITH

Jesus answered and said to them, "This is the work of God, that you believe in the one he sent."

John 6:29, NAB

Reflection:

God works. According to this Scripture, God works so that we will believe in the One that He sent—Jesus. God's work is that of invitation. God invites each person into a relationship with Him.

The Church teaches us that when we have faith in God, we are led to depend on Him alone and that nothing else will be able to take his place. (CCC 229)

We are to prefer God and not let anything substitute for Him. In this world, it is easy to become distracted, to follow many things, and to believe in many causes; yet God is working to invite us into a relationship with Him and an understanding that we are to prefer Him to earthly pleasures.

Our daily lives offer us many distractions and contain many responsibilities. We may have children to get to school, parents to take care of, or a job to do; however, we are called into a relationship with God and we must treasure that relationship first. Regardless of our other commitments, our faith demands that we put God first. From the moment we wake up in the morning, God should be our first thought and He should determine our actions throughout the day.

Contemplation Question(s):

Whom did God send? Why is it a work of God that we believe in the One that He sent?

Personal Reflection:

Do you believe in the One that God sent? Why or why not? How does that belief change how you live your life?

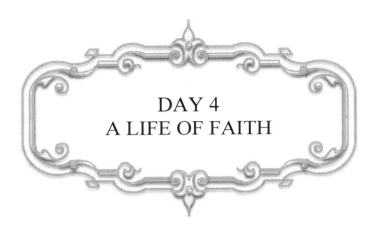

DAY 4
A LIFE OF FAITH

Abram put his faith in the
LORD, who attributed it to him
as an act of righteousness.

Genesis 15:6, NAB

Reflection:

Righteousness means that you are acting in alignment with God's will. Abram was just a man going about his life when God introduced Himself and asked Abram to follow Him. God changed Abram's name to Abraham because when Abraham decided to follow God and have faith in God, the reality of who he was and what he would do was changed—the old became new. Abraham was a "new creation." God had made Abraham into a "father of a multitude of nations." (Genesis 17:5)

When we accept God's invitation and have faith in Him alone, we are made into new creations—we are no longer the sinful people that we were with no hope, we are cleansed and able to have an ongoing relationship with God. Although we still sin, we have the opportunity to ask for God's forgiveness and receive His mercy and grace.

Contemplation Question(s):

God accepted Abraham's faith as an act of righteousness. What is righteousness? Why is it important? What does it mean to put your faith in the Lord?

Personal Reflection:

Do you place your faith in the Lord? How? Is it a daily act for you?

DEACON LARRY ONEY

DAY 5
FOLLOWING
THE FAITH

For this reason, it depends on faith, so that it may be a gift, and the promise may be guaranteed to all his descendants, not to those who only adhere to the law but to those who follow the faith of Abraham, who is the father of all of us.

Romans 4:16, NAB

Reflection:

In the early church, Christians were required to memorize the Creed—the statement of faith. Today, Christians still memorize the Creed and profess their belief in it at every Sunday. The Nicene Creed (and the Apostle's Creed) is a profession of faith that Christians repeat as a way to state what they believe in and to declare their faith in God.

Every time Christians profess the Creed, they are stating that they are in unity with the Christian Church and stating exactly what they believe as a Christian—it is a witness to their faith—a declaration and a call to others to join the faith that they profess.

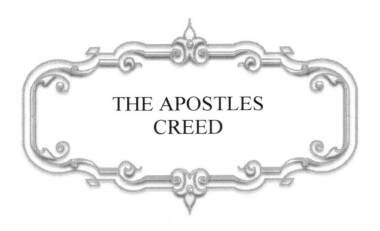

THE APOSTLES CREED

I believe in God, the Father Almighty, Creator of
Heaven and earth;
and in Jesus Christ, His only Son Our Lord,
Who was conceived by the Holy Spirit, born of the
Virgin Mary, suffered under Pontius Pilate, was
crucified, died, and was buried.
He descended into Hell; the third day He rose again
from the dead;
He ascended into Heaven, and sitteth at the right
hand of God, the Father almighty; from thence He
shall come to judge the living and the dead.
I believe in the Holy Spirit, the holy Catholic
Church, the communion of saints, the forgiveness of
sins, the resurrection of the body and life everlasting.
Amen.

THE NICENE CREED

I believe in one God,
the Father almighty,
maker of heaven and earth,
of all things visible and invisible.

I believe in one Lord Jesus Christ,
the Only Begotten Son of God,
born of the Father before all ages.
God from God, Light from Light,
true God from true God,
begotten, not made, consubstantial with the Father;
through him all things were made.
For us men and for our salvation
he came down from heaven,
and by the Holy Spirit was incarnate of the Virgin
Mary,
and became man.

For our sake he was crucified under Pontius Pilate,
he suffered death and was buried,
and rose again on the third day
in accordance with the Scriptures.
He ascended into heaven
and is seated at the right hand of the Father.
He will come again in glory
to judge the living and the dead
and his kingdom will have no end.

I believe in the Holy Spirit, the Lord, the giver of
life,
who proceeds from the Father and the Son,
who with the Father and the Son is adored and
glorified,
who has spoken through the prophets.

I believe in one, holy, catholic and apostolic Church.
I confess one Baptism for the forgiveness of sins
and I look forward to the resurrection of the dead
and the life of the world to come. Amen.

Contemplation Question(s):

What is the "faith of Abraham?" How does one follow this faith? Why is Abraham a father to us all?

Personal Reflection:

Faith is a gift—have you "opened" this gift? Do you use this gift?

DAY 6
ESTHER FAITH

Esther sent back to Mordecai the response: "Go and assemble all the Jews who are in Susa; fast on my behalf, all of you, not eating or drinking night or day for three days. I and my maids will also fast in the same way. Thus prepared, I will go to the king, contrary to the law. If I perish, I perish!"

Esther 4:15-16, NAB

Reflection:

The Book of Esther is an exciting tale of one woman's call to faith and her response. Esther was a Jewish woman married to a Persian King (he did not know that she was Jewish). At that time, a person could not go to see the king unless he called for that person—it could mean that person's death to do otherwise.

Mordecai, Esther's uncle, told her that the king had declared that all Jews would be killed at a certain time and asked her to intervene. Esther put her faith in God and asked Mordecai and the Jews in the city to fast and pray for her for three days. Esther knew the power of prayer and fasting and she had faith in God that He would hear their plea and keep her safe. Through her faith, and the faith of the Jewish people, not only did Esther survive going to see the king uninvited, but she help to save all of the Jews in that kingdom (the declaration to kill all of the Jews was lifted by the king).

Contemplation Question(s):

How did Esther show her faith?

Personal Reflection:

Do you feel like your faith is strong enough to stand for what is right no matter the consequences? How do you prepare yourself for what is to come in daily life? Do you pray and fast as an act of faith?

DEACON LARRY ONEY

PART TWO:

Faith
as a Gift
from God

DAY 7
GIFT OF FAITH

For by grace you have been saved through faith, and this is not from you; it is the gift of God.

Ephesians 2:8, NAB

Reflection:

Our good God is a Giver of Gifts. The Father sent Jesus, Jesus sent the Holy Spirit, and the Holy Spirit continually gives us those gifts we need to draw nearer to God, The Father.

Faith is a gift from The Father, an invitation to know Him. Faith is also a gift from Jesus—it is a gift to believe and follow Him. Faith is also a gift of the Holy Spirit—a gift that strengthens us and our belief in God—Father, Son, and Holy Spirit. (See 1 Corinthians 12:4-11)

The Church declares that "Faith is a supernatural gift from God. In order to believe, man needs the interior helps of the Holy Spirit." (CCC 179)

It is by God's grace that we are saved when we have faith in Jesus and the One who sent Him.

Contemplation Question(s):

What is grace?

Personal Reflection:

Faith is a gift from God—Father, Son, and Holy Spirit. St. Paul lists the gifts in 1 Corinthians 12:4-11 as: wisdom, knowledge, faith, healing, mighty deeds, prophecy, discernment of spirits, tongues, and interpretation of tongues. What gifts of the Holy Spirit are you using on a daily basis?

DEACON LARRY ONEY

DAY 8
FAITH HEARING

Thus faith comes from what is heard, and what is heard comes through the word of Christ.

Romans 10:17, NAB

Reflection:

The Scripture is the Word of God. The Bible indicated that faith comes by what is heard. When we listen to the Word of God, read the Word of God, and contemplate the Word of God, we are learning more about our faith and the One who gives us our faith.

Reading and learning Scripture is an important part of the Christian's spiritual journey. We must know what we profess to believe in before we can truly profess to believe. What we listen to has an effect on us. One of the weapons that the Enemy uses against the Body of Christ is by getting us to listen to (hear) things that tear down the dignity of the human person and that attacks the Word of Truth that lives in the Word of God. As Christians, we must guard what we listen to—as the world has a message and the Word of God has a message as well.

Contemplation Question(s):

How does faith come from what is heard?

Personal Reflection:

Are you sensitive to not listening to things that the world offers that might adversely affect the way you walk with the Lord? How often do you listen (or read) the Word of God?

DEACON LARRY ONEY

DAY 9
FAITH WALK

So, as you received Christ
Jesus the Lord, walk in him,
rooted in him and built upon
him and established in the faith
as you were taught, abounding
in thanksgiving.

Colossians 2:6-7, NAB

Reflection:

Faith is established through Christ. The Word of God calls us to build our faith on Jesus and stay rooted in Him. The writers of Scripture often used natural references to help people understand spiritual truths.

Another natural reference used by Jesus can be found in John 15:4-5:

> Remain in me, as I remain in you. Just as a branch cannot bear fruit on its own unless it remains on the vine, so neither can you unless you remain in me. I am the vine, you are the branches. Whoever remains in me and I in him will bear much fruit, because without me you can do nothing. (NAB)

As Christians, we are called to stay connected to Christ and to draw our strength and nourishment from Him alone—like branches and roots on a tree. We are to root ourselves in Christ. That means that we are to be fed by Christ—the Bread of Life and the Word of God. By hearing and taking in what Jesus taught, sharing in His life, death, and Resurrection, we are grounded in our faith—that which we profess to be true. Jesus is the Bread of Life:

> Jesus said to them, "I am the bread of life; whoever comes to me will never hunger, and whoever believes in me will never thirst. (John 6:35, NAB)

When we go to Mass and partake of the Eucharist, it is a celebration of what was and what is to come.

We are dying and rising with Him, we are remembering The Last Supper and all that followed, in the hope that Jesus will come again. That's why we sing, "We Remember" by Marty Haugen: "We remember how you loved us to your death, and still we celebrate, for you are with us here; And we believe that we will see you when you come, in your glory, Lord, we remember, we celebrate, we believe."

Contemplation Question(s):

What does Colossians 2:6-7 teach us about how we are to "root" ourselves in Christ to build up our faith?

Personal Reflection:

Is your spiritual foundation rooted in Christ— are you connected to Christ as a branch is to a vine? What "pruning" do you need to do?

DAY 10
FAITH PRAYER

But you, beloved, build yourselves up in your most holy faith; pray in the holy Spirit.

Jude 1:20, NAB

Reflection:

St. Paul was very clear in his writings that he prayed using the gift of tongues (praying in the Holy Spirit) so that he would be built up and strengthened in his faith (see 1 Corinthians 14:18). In Jude 1:20, we are again taught to pray in the Holy Spirit—that will help to build our faith.

Prayer is an important key to a healthy spiritual life. Prayer is a conversation with God. By allowing the Holy Spirit to pray through us, we are able to pray as we ought—to pray about what is truly important. But as St. Paul warns, it is not just that we are letting the Spirit pray through us, we are also praying with our mind and being an active participant in the prayer. (See 1 Corinthians 14:13-19)

Contemplation Question(s):

Why do Christians need to continually build up in their faith? How does prayer help to build us up?

Personal Reflection:

Do you pray in tongues? Why or why not?

DEACON LARRY ONEY

DAY 11
SAFEGUARDING FAITH

Blessed be the God and Father of our Lord Jesus Christ, who in his great mercy gave us a new birth to a living hope through the resurrection of Jesus Christ from the dead, to an inheritance that is imperishable, undefiled, and unfading, kept in heaven for you who by the power of God are safeguarded through faith, to a salvation that is ready to be revealed in the final time.

1 Peter 1:3-5, NAB

Reflection:

This Scripture speaks of our being safeguarded by our faith. Faith guards us and keeps us safe. How does that work?

When the arrows of the Enemy are coming straight at us, it is our faith that reminds us of our eternal hope. Our faith reminds us of our "inheritance that is imperishable, undefiled, and unfading" that awaits us in Heaven. (see 1 Peter 1:4) Amen! Hallelujah!

Our inheritance in Heaven, given to us by God, through faith, cannot perish—it cannot rust or fade. Through our faith we are saved and protected.

Contemplation Question(s):

This Scripture is a blessing of God for His kindness and mercy. When was the last time you reflected and contemplated on God's mercy and grace in your life?

Personal Reflection:

When you are under attack by the enemy, what do you rely on?

DEACON LARRY ONEY

DAY 12
SAUL/PAUL FAITH

On his journey, as he was
nearing Damascus, a light from
the sky suddenly flashed
around him. He fell to the
ground and heard a voice
saying to him, "Saul, Saul, why
are you persecuting me?" He
said, "Who are you, sir?" The
reply came, "I am Jesus, whom
you are persecuting.

Now get up and go into the city and you will be told what you must do."

Acts 9:3-6, NAB

Reflection:

This Scripture passage, along with Acts 9:7-30, tell the story of Paul's conversion to the faith. Here was a man that was trying to stop the spread of faith in Christ by killing Christians. Then Paul had an experience with Jesus—Paul saw the risen Jesus and heard His voice. On that day, Paul received his faith! From that moment on, Paul's life was not easy. He had enjoyed a prominent place in society and was well-respected; yet he gave that all up to follow Jesus. Paul's life was forever changed by his encounter with the Risen Lord Jesus. Paul went where the Holy Spirit led him and preached to all who would stand still long enough to hear his words.

Today, we too can experience the Risen Lord Jesus—we can hear His Word through the Bible, we can experience Him through the Communion feast, we can serve Him through our service to others, and we can follow Him by following the prompting of the Holy Spirit.

Contemplation Question(s):

Saul was traveling to find more Christians to kill when he saw and heard a vision of Jesus. Jesus asked one question of Saul, "why are you persecuting me?" What effect did this one question have on Saul's life and the Christian Church?

Personal Reflection:

Have you ever been asked one question that changed your life? Have you had an authentic encounter with the Risen Christ and if so, what effect has it had on your life? If not, what plans do you to change that?

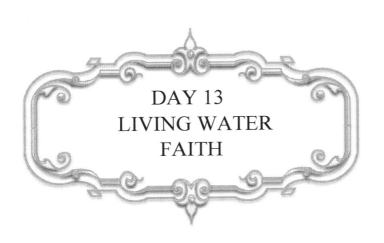

DAY 13
LIVING WATER
FAITH

So he came to a town of Samaria called Sychar, near the plot of land that Jacob had given to his son Joseph. Jacob's well was there. Jesus, tired from his journey, sat down there at the well. It was about noon. A woman of Samaria came to draw water. Jesus said to her, "Give me a drink." His disciples had gone into the town to buy food. The

Samaritan woman said to him, "How can you, a Jew, ask me, a Samaritan woman, for a drink?" (For Jews use nothing in common with Samaritans.) Jesus answered and said to her, "If you knew the gift of God and who is saying to you, 'Give me a drink,' you would have asked him and he would have given you living water."

John 4:5-10, NAB

Reflection:

The woman by the well is a familiar story to many people. Jesus engages the woman as she is doing one of her daily activities and he does so through speech and invites her to serve Him; yet He also offers her a way to encounter Him so that she could be gifted with "living water."

Jesus knew that the woman at the well needed living water—something that would change her life and sustain her through the difficulties of life; and He found a way to open the dialogue with her so that He could provide for her. Faith gives us the courage to go to God and ask for what we need. Faith reminds us of who we are in Christ—even when life is at its roughest. Faith is a gift that opens the door to all of God's gifts. Faith gave the woman the courage to respond. If we continue with this passage further, we notice that in John 4:28-42, the woman left the well and went to tell the townspeople about Jesus and they also came to believe in Jesus. Her faith would not let her be silent.

Contemplation Question(s):

In this Scripture, Jesus gives the woman at the well access to Living Water. What is the Living Water?

Personal Reflection:

When did your invitation to Jesus come and how did you respond? How has your response to Jesus changed over time? Are you still excited to know Jesus?

PART THREE:

Faith
as an Act
Toward God

DEACON LARRY ONEY

DAY 14
HAVING FAITH

"Do not let your hearts be troubled. You have faith in God; have faith also in me."

John 14:1, NAB

Reflection:

This is a Scripture that we unusually hear at funerals to give consolation to those who have had a loved one die.

Jesus pointed out that faith will keep our hearts from being troubled. Having faith in God means that we believe what God has said in His Word and through His actions.

God's Word says that God has good things planned for us. (See Jeremiah 29:11) The enemy wants us to believe that everything is going wrong; but Jesus brings us peace—a peace that surpasses all understanding (see Philippians 4:7). God's gifts work together—faith and peace and love.

Contemplation Question(s):

How can faith in God keep our heart from being troubled?

Personal Reflection:

Do you get easily upset at things that happen around you? How can your faith help you to not let your heart be troubled?

DEACON LARRY ONEY

DAY 15
HEALING FAITH

There was a woman afflicted
with hemorrhages for twelve years.
She had suffered greatly at the
hands of many doctors and had
spent all that she had. Yet she was
not helped but only grew worse.
She had heard about Jesus and
came up behind him in the crowd
and touched his cloak. She said,
"If I but touch his clothes, I shall
be cured." Immediately her flow of
blood dried up. She felt in her body
that she was healed of her

affliction. Jesus, aware at once that power had gone out from him, turned around in the crowd and asked, "Who has touched my clothes?" But his disciples said to him, "You see how the crowd is pressing upon you, and yet you ask, 'Who touched me?'" And he looked around to see who had done it. The woman, realizing what had happened to her, approached in fear and trembling. She fell down before Jesus and told him the whole truth. He said to her, "Daughter, your faith has saved you. Go in peace and be cured of your affliction."

Mark 5:25-34, NAB

Reflection:

This is one of the great Scriptures of the Bible about faith and healing! This woman had suffered for so long and had tried so many different cures and saw many different doctors. After years of struggle, her faith in anything would have been surprising. And yet, when she heard that Jesus was going to walk through her town, she had such faith in Him that she was willing to go against the Jewish social customs of the day just to touch the hem of His garment. She didn't even want to speak to Him— her faith told her that was not necessary—she just wanted to touch the hem of his garment. What faith!

Not only did Jesus heal her, He gifted her with speech—He spoke to her, something she probably treasured for the rest of her life. Jesus did not call her out or try to embarrass her or rebuke her; rather He loved her and healed her.

It is remarkable too that Jesus gave her peace because of her faith in Him. Her faith led to her to Jesus. Jesus healed her and gave her peace.

Contemplation Question(s):

The sick woman told Jesus the whole truth when asked. What kind of faith did this woman possess?

Personal Reflection:

Do you have the faith of the sick woman to go to Jesus? Are you willing to be healed by Jesus of whatever is afflicting you? Said another way, the woman in the Scripture had an issue of blood—what is the issue that you might need Jesus to touch in your life?

CHAPTER 16
STRENGTHENING
FAITH

They strengthened the spirits
of the disciples and exhorted
them to persevere in the faith,
saying, "It is necessary for us to
undergo many hardships to
enter the kingdom of God."
They appointed presbyters for
them in each church and, with
prayer and fasting, commended
them to the Lord in whom they
had put their faith.

Acts 14:22-23, NAB

Reflection:

In this Scripture, Luke is pointing out the difficulty of persevering in the faith—it is an action that requires time and attention. There are things that need to be done in order to build up our faith so that we can persevere during times of trouble and hardship. Life in this world can be difficult, but that does not mean that we have to lose your precious gift of faith.

We must cling to our faith. We must renew our faith daily and participate in those activities that will help to build our faith and avoid those things that might damage our faith.

The Church teaches, "The first commandment requires us to nourish and protect our faith with prudence and vigilance, and to reject everything that is opposed to it…" (CCC 2088)

Contemplation Question(s):

What does it mean to persevere in the faith?

Personal Reflection:

What do you do to build up your faith so that you can persevere in the faith? (Do you pray, fast, read your Bible, belong to a spiritual growth group, or write in a journal what God has done for you?)

DEACON LARRY ONEY

DAY 17
BLIND FAITH

As he passed by he saw a man blind from birth. His disciples asked him, "Rabbi, who sinned, this man or his parents, that he was born blind?" Jesus answered, "Neither he nor his parents sinned; it is so that the works of God might be made visible through him. We have to do the works of the one who sent me while it is day. Night is coming when no one can work. While I am in the world, I am the light of the world." When he had said this, he spat on the ground and made clay with the saliva, and smeared the clay on his eyes, and said to him, "Go wash in the Pool of Siloam" (which means Sent). So he went and washed, and came back able to see.

John 9:1-7, NAB

Reflection:

People around us can sometimes want someone to blame for what goes wrong in life. In the case of the man born blind, Jesus states clearly that no one sinned or did anything wrong. Through this man, God's works would be made visible to the world.

Every Christian, at one time or another, is asked why bad things happen in this world? The Church points out that, "There is not a single aspect of the Christian message that is not in part an answer to the question of evil." (CCC 309)

That means that if you want a simple answer, then you will be disappointed. The entire Christian message, from God revealing Himself to His people to Jesus dying and being Resurrected contains some part of that answer to why bad things happen in the world. Bad things happen in this world— sometimes we know why and sometimes things don't make sense to us in our finite human understanding. Under all circumstances, we should persevere in our faith and continue to believe God.

Contemplation Question(s):

Jesus spit in the dirt and smeared this mixture on the man's eyes and then told the man to go and wash. What was the result?

Personal Reflection:

Do you obey Jesus's instructions?

DAY 18
FIRM FAITH

Be on your guard, stand firm in the faith, be courageous, be strong. Your every act should be done with love.

1 Corinthians 16:13-14, NAB

Reflection:

Many Christians today know that they must stand firm in the faith like this Scripture instructs; unfortunately, some do not do so with love.

It is important to remember that when we are standing up for our faith that we are to be witnesses of Jesus and do so lovingly as He did. This Scripture tells us that our every act should be done with love— not just acts for our family or when we are choosing to do service for someone, but **every** act!

Contemplation Question(s):

Why does a Christian have to be on guard?

Personal Reflection:

Do you stand up for your faith? Is your every act done with love?

DEACON LARRY ONEY

DAY 19
EXCEL IN FAITH

Now as you excel in every
respect, in faith, discourse,
knowledge, all earnestness, and
in the love we have for you,
may you excel in this gracious
act also.

2 Corinthians 8:7, NAB

Reflection:

Here St. Paul speaks about one's faith leading to service. Because we have faith, we feel moved to serve. When we serve those in need, we are serving Jesus. As we grow in our faith, we come to realize that Jesus came to serve—He came to save us.

As followers of Jesus, we too are called into service of others. The Holy Spirit prompts us to serve according to our gifts. A teacher is compelled to teach. One gifted with healing is compelled to heal. If you are called to preach—you should preach.

> "But how can they call on him in whom they have not believed? And how can they believe in him of whom they have not heard? And how can they hear without someone to preach?" (Romans 10:14, NAB)

A person with the gift of administration feels called to serve by organizing events or helping others in their ministries.

Contemplation Question(s):

How does faith lead to service?

Personal Reflection:

How do you serve others?

DEACON LARRY ONEY

DAY 20
GROUNDED FAITH

And you who once were
alienated and hostile in mind
because of evil deeds he has
now reconciled in his fleshly
body through his death, to
present you holy, without
blemish, and irreproachable
before him, provided that you
persevere in the faith, firmly
grounded, stable, and not
shifting from the hope of the
gospel that you heard, which

has been preached to every
creature under heaven, of
which I, Paul, am a minister.

Colossians 1:21-23, NAB

Reflection:

We have spoken of persevering in the faith already, but let's take that a step further. This Scripture passage speaks of "not shifting from the hope of the gospel." Sometimes we try to ride the fence and not be on either side of a debate.

We are not in a debate—we are at war! There is God's Kingdom and the Kingdom of Darkness and you are either on one side or the other. There is no time for waffling—this is the time of decisive action. Which side are you on?

Contemplation Question(s):

How can a Christian stay firmly grounded and not shift from the hope of the Gospel?

Personal Reflection:

How do you stay firmly grounded? What side are you on in this battle?

DAY 21
FIGHTING FAITH

I entrust this charge to you,
Timothy, my child, in
accordance with the prophetic
words once spoken about you.
Through them may you fight a
good fight by having faith and
a good conscience. Some, by
rejecting conscience, have
made a shipwreck of their faith.

1 Timothy 1:18-19, NAB

Reflection:

Timothy was charged with a task by Paul in accordance to the prophetic words spoken over him. Paul then told Timothy that in order to carry out his calling, he would have to keep his faith and a good conscience. Paul links a good conscience with a strong faith.

What does one have to do with the other? Faith is about obedience to God and God's will for your life. When we do something that is against God's will, then we are rejecting our consciences—that part of us that tells us right from wrong.

Our conscience guides us to not only do what is right over what is wrong, it also urges us to do something rather than to do nothing.

Contemplation Question(s):

How does rejecting one's conscience lead to shipwrecking his/her faith?

Personal Reflection:

Do you have a good conscience?

DEACON LARRY ONEY

DAY 22
FAITH TOWARD OTHERS

Beloved, you are faithful in all you do for the brothers, especially for strangers; they have testified to your love before the church. Please help them in a way worthy of God to continue their journey.

3 John 1:5-6, NAB

ʾtion:

As we travel our own journey of faith, we are called to evangelize and help others on their journey of faith—whether they are at the beginning of their faith journey or close to the end of their earthly life.

This scripture passage teaches us that it truly does build our faith to help others on their own journey. It is not about telling others what to do; rather it is about sharing, demonstrating, caring, and listening to others as we are led by the Holy Spirit.

.

Contemplation Question(s):

What are some ways that are "worthy of God" to help others continue their faith journey?

Personal Reflection:

What are some ways that you can help others on their faith journey? What are some things that you can do to help others on their faith journey?

.

DEACON LARRY ONEY

DAY 23
FAITH IN ACTION

In charge of the storerooms I appointed Shelemiah the priest, Zadok the scribe, and Pedaiah, one of the Levites, together with Hanan, son of Zaccur, son of Mattaniah, as their assistant; for they were considered trustworthy. It was their duty to make the distribution to their kinsmen.

Nehemiah 13:13, NAB

Reflection:

We are called to work together toward different goals in life and to be trustworthy in all that we do. Part of being faithful is being trustworthy. Jesus often spoke of people being trustworthy in the parables and what the consequences were when they were not trustworthy.

When others are depending on us, it is important that we do what we asked to do and to do it in a fair and just way. As Christians we represent Christ—our actions are evaluated by those around us and we are judged by them (sometimes more harshly because of our profession of faith).

Contemplation Question(s):

Why is being trustworthy important?

Personal Reflection:

Are you trustworthy with everyone you come into contact with on a daily basis?

DEACON LARRY ONEY

"Who, then, is the faithful and prudent servant, whom the master has put in charge of his household to distribute to them their food at the proper time? Blessed is that servant whom his master on his arrival finds doing so. Amen, I say to you, he will put him in charge of all his property. But if that wicked servant says to himself, 'My master is long delayed,' and begins to beat his fellow servants, and eat and drink with drunkards, the servant's master will come on an unexpected day and at an unknown hour and will punish him severely.

Matthew 24:45-51a, NAB

Reflection:

In accordance with our calling by God, we all have jobs to do and a set time to do them. When Jesus returns (or when our time on this earth is over), what will He discover?

When we stand face to face with God and we are being judged, what will He say to us? I pray that He says, "Well done, my good and faithful servant." (See Matthew 25:23).

Contemplation Question(s):

What do the two servants in this Scripture passage do and what are the consequences?

Personal Reflection:

What are you called to do? Are you doing it?

DAY 25
SHIELDING FAITH

In all circumstances, hold faith as a shield, to quench all [the] flaming arrows of the evil one."

Ephesians 6:16, NAB

Reflection:

If someone were to sit down and draw a picture of a shield to use in battle, what would that person draw? Would that person draw a big solid shield that was thick and easy to get a good grip? Or would the drawing be of a small shield full of holes with no firm grip?

Obviously, if we were going into battle, we would want a shield that we could firmly grip, that would be of sturdy construction, and that would withstand the enemy's attacks. This Scripture passage is comparing our faith to a shield. It is imperative that we evaluate our faith on a regular basis and decide how we are working with the Holy Spirit to build up our faith and make our shield stronger. There are many ways that we can build up our faith and make our shield stronger. We could participate in Bible study, attend a conference, join a prayer group, or commit to using the gifts of the Holy Spirit on a daily basis.

Contemplation Question(s):

How can faith be a shield?

Personal Reflection:

Do you hold your faith as a shield? What do you do to build up your faith?

DEACON LARRY ONEY

DAY 26
STANDING FAITH

Now Stephen, filled with grace and power, was working great wonders and signs among the people.

Acts 6:8, NAB

Reflection:

Acts, chapters 6 and 7 describe Stephen's teachings and his martyrdom. Acts 6:15 points out that those who were looking at Stephen noticed that "his face was like the face of an angel" while he was speaking about Jesus. (NAB)

A change came over Stephen when he was speaking to others—even his enemies. When Stephen spoke of Jesus, Jesus was able to shine through him and others could see.

Faith really can change the way a person looks or speaks. During my first professional job, I knew a man who was very religious—a real man of faith. He was a simple man. He worked hard and had a real love for the Lord. He was kind to others and always spoke, but he had a terrible stuttering problem. One day, a few of us were standing around chatting during lunch and the Bible came up. This man, who was known to have a stuttering problem, amazed us all when he began to speak of the Lord and the Bible—his face was serene and he spoke with conviction, without stuttering once! He shared his faith and his human limitations did not get in the way once for this man of faith. Praise God!

Today, when Christians speak of Jesus, can you see a difference about them as they speak the name of Jesus? When you speak and teach about Jesus, do you feel different? Stephen spoke from a pure heart, a heart full of love for those he was speaking to, even if they didn't believe him—he still loved them.

Contemplation Question(s):

According to this Scripture, how was Stephen working great wonders and signs?

Personal Reflection:

How is God's grace and power being used in your life? Do you believe that God can work great wonders and signs through you?

And the apostles said to the Lord, "Increase our faith." The Lord replied, "If you have faith the size of a mustard seed, you would say to [this] mulberry tree, 'Be uprooted and planted in the sea,' and it would obey you.

Luke 17:5-6, NAB

Reflection:

A mustard seed is the size of a speck, barely noticeable. If you look away from it and then look back, you might misplace it. This Scripture always challenges my faith to grow. What do we have faith in and what do we do with our faith? This passage of Scripture seems to indicate that we are supposed to do things with our faith—that faith has use and should be used for a purpose. Why do we have faith?

The apostles asked for more faith. This is incredible! The very men who traveled with Jesus, spoke face to face with Jesus, and saw all that Jesus said and did and they asked for more faith. If they recognized the need for more faith, shouldn't we also recognize not only our need for more faith, but also for wisdom and understanding on what to do with the faith that we have.

Contemplation Question(s):

Why did the apostles ask for more faith?

Personal Reflection:

What do you do with your faith? What are some positive ways that you could use your faith? Do you need more faith? Have you asked God to give you more faith?

DEACON LARRY ONEY

DAY 28
TRUST AND FAITH

On this account I am suffering
these things; but I am not
ashamed, for I know him in
whom I have believed and am
confident that he is able to guard
what has been entrusted to me
until that day. Take as your norm
the sound words that you heard
from me, in the faith and love
that are in Christ Jesus. Guard
this rich trust with the help of the
holy Spirit that dwells within us.

2 Timothy 1:12-14, NAB

Reflection:

Let's focus on the fact that Paul writes that he is "confident that he is able to guard what has been entrusted to me until that day." The "he" here is Jesus. Paul is saying that he is confident that Jesus is able to guard what has been entrusted to Paul until Paul is able to resume his duties.

In today's world, it is easy to believe that if we are not the one doing whatever it is we do, then things will fall apart or be done wrong or the message won't get out there. Yet, here is Paul—a person who spread the Gospel message far and wide—who is admitting that if something stops him for a while, everything will be okay because Jesus has it all under control.

God knows what is going to happen—there are no surprises to God. God has a plan and while He would like for us to cooperate with that plan, He also has it covered when we are not able. In the words of a good friend of mine, Bill Mitchell, "Jesus is the Master and the Master has a Master Plan, so we don't have to worry." This also speaks to what we discussed on Day 14—we must keep our peace. God has things under control and we don't have to know every detail or to be in control. In fact, we are called to let God be in control and just follow the Spirit with trust and peace.

Contemplation Question(s):

What does St. Paul tell us to guard and how should we guard it?

Personal Reflection:

Do you guard your faith? Do you rely on God to be in control?

DAY 29
FRUITFUL FAITH

The fruit of the Spirit is love,
joy, peace, patience, kindness,
generosity, faithfulness.

Galatians 5:22b, NAB

Reflection:

One of the fruits of the Spirit is faithfulness. The phrase "fruit of the Spirit" refers to what is the result of something that you do. If you hold a prayer group in your home, what is the result? If people grow in the Word and grow closer to God and each other, then that is "good fruit." However, if people begin to fight and they stop going to church as a result of being in that group, then that is "bad fruit."

Sometimes we can do "good" things, but no fruit is seen right away. That doesn't mean that our actions will not one day bear fruit, perhaps we were just planting a seed that another will water. Having faith means that when you are called to do something, you do it as you were instructed to do to the best of your ability and then trust God to bring about the good fruit in His time. As St. Paul says, some plant, some water, but it is God who gives the increase. (1 Corinthians 3:5-9)

Contemplation Question(s):

How does one produce good fruit in the spiritual realm?

Personal Reflection:

What good fruit have you produced lately? How?

DEACON LARRY ONEY

DAY 30
SUPPLEMENT FAITH

For this very reason, make every effort to supplement your faith with virtue, virtue with knowledge, knowledge with self-control, self-control with endurance, endurance with devotion, devotion with mutual affection, mutual affection with love. If these are yours and increase in abundance, they will keep you from being idle or unfruitful in the knowledge of our Lord Jesus Christ.

2 Peter 1:5-8, NAB

Reflection:

Notice that to increase one's faith, we must supplement it with virtue. To improve our virtue, we must supplement it with knowledge, and so on. This speaks to the fact that God is a God of order. All good things come from God and He uses them to help us grow closer to Him—Father, Son, and Holy Spirit.

As we increase our faith, virtue, knowledge, self-control, endurance, devotion, mutual affection, and love, we are kept from being idle or unfruitful. So, just by growing in these virtues and gifts, we will not be idle, we will be active participants in God's army and we will bear good fruit!

Contemplation Question(s):

How do we supplement our faith?

Personal Reflection:

What areas do you need to grow in more fully from the list of virtues in this Scripture?

One man was there who had been ill for thirty-eight years. When Jesus saw him lying there and knew that he had been ill for a long time, he said to him, "Do you want to be well?" The sick man answered him, "Sir, I have no one to put me into the pool when the water is stirred up; while I am on my way, someone else gets down there before me." Jesus said to him, "Rise, take up your mat, and walk." Immediately the man became well, took up his mat, and walked.

John 5:5-9a, NAB

Reflection:

One of the most profound questions that Jesus ever asks is found in this passage—"Do you want to be well?" As Christians, we have to realize that not everyone wants to be healed of their illness—whether physical, emotional, or spiritual. Jesus loves them just as they are and we are called to love them as well. This man wanted to be healed but could not see how to accomplish this on his own.

We do not have to do anything alone in this world because Jesus is with us. Jesus wants to help us—Jesus loves us! Notice that Jesus did not put the man in the water, which is what the man thought he needed; rather Jesus made a declaration—"Rise, take up your mat, and walk." And the man obeyed. Obedience to Jesus takes faith and the man showed his faith by getting up and walking—he did not doubt that he would be able to walk because Jesus said to do it, therefore he knew that he would be able to walk.

When Jesus asks us to do something, we are equipped to do whatever it is He told us to do—our faith teaches us that. So, when the world says, "You can't do that," we know that is a falsehood because Jesus declared that we could. We must use our faith to listen to Jesus, to rely on Jesus, to trust Jesus, and to obey Him. Jesus loves us and He wants to heal us of all of our brokenness and it is our faith that helps us to accept that healing!

Contemplation Question(s):

What did Jesus ask of the man and how did the man respond? What was the outcome?

Personal Reflection:

How can you grow in your faith? How can your faith help you to answer the call of Jesus?

For More information about Deacon Larry Oney and his ministry, please go to:

www.LarryOney.com

And be sure to read Deacon Larry's Inspiring Testimony:

Available at Amazon.com and other bookstores.

And be sure to read
Deacon Larry's other
Reflection Book:

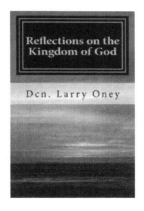

Available at Amazon.com
and other bookstores.

ABOUT THE AUTHOR

Deacon Larry D. Oney is a Permanent Deacon for the Diocese of New Orleans, Louisiana. He is assigned to Saint Louis King of France Cathedral in the historic French Quarter in New Orleans. He and his family reside in LaPlace, Louisiana and are members of Our Lady of Grace Catholic Church. Larry is the Chairman of the Board of Hammerman & Gainer, Inc. (HGI), and a member of the New Orleans Chapter of Legatus. He also serves as the Chairman of the Board of Regents for Our Lady of Holy Cross College. Mr. Oney is on the Advisory Board of Vatican Capital, as well as an investor.

Deacon Oney recently published his first book, *Amazing Grace Overcoming Race*, in which he shares his struggles with racism as he grew up as a sharecropper's son in Louisiana and God's love and grace in his life! His second book, *Reflections on the Kingdom of God* was released in January of 2013.

Deacon Larry ministers internationally and has appeared on EWTN, Franciscan Radio, Ava Maria Radio, and FOCUS TV. Deacon Larry has a dynamic ministry of preaching, teaching, and exhortation. He utilizes humor, Sacred Scripture, and his love for the people of God, to speak to the heart of God's people in an uplifting manner. For more information about Deacon Larry Oney and his ministry, please visit his webpage at: www.LarryOney.com.

22472431R00080

Made in the USA
Columbia, SC
01 August 2018